Before the tunnel closed behind you forever,
was your last thought of heaven?
Of the life you lived here?
...Was it of me?

~ Kaylie Rose

(Excerpt from "The After" pg. 31)

Also by Kaylie Rose

Reflecting the Sky (Silver Bow Publishing)

Reflecting the Sunset

by

Kaylie Rose

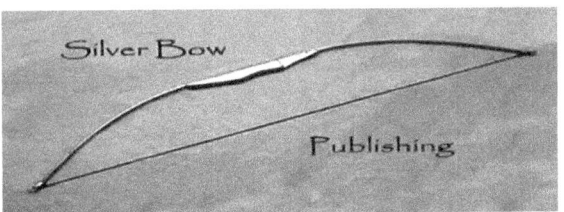

720 Sixth Street, Unit # 5
New Westminster, BC
CANADA V3L 3C5

Title: Reflecting the Sunset
Author: Kaylie Rose
Cover Photo: "Misty Morning Lights" painting by Candice James
Layout and Design: Candice James
Editor: Candice James

All rights reserved including the right to reproduce or translate this book or any portions thereof, in any form without the permission of the publisher. Except for the use of short passages for review purposes, no part of this book may be reproduced, in part or in whole, or transmitted in any form or by any means, electronically or mechanically, including photocopying, recording, or any information or storage retrieval system without prior permission in writing from the publisher or a licence from the Canadian Copyright Collective Agency (Access Copyright).

www.silverbowpublishing.com
© Silver Bow Publishing
info@silverbowpublishing.com

ISBN: 9781774033661 print
ISBN: 9781774033678 e book

Library and Archives Canada Cataloguing in Publication

Title: Reflecting the sunset / by Kaylie Rose.
Names: Rose, Kaylie, author.
Identifiers: Canadiana (print) 20250211823 | Canadiana (ebook) 20250215373 | ISBN 9781774033661
   (softcover) | ISBN 9781774033678 (Kindle)
Subjects: LCGFT: Poetry.
Classification: LCC PS3618.O795 R46 2025 | DDC 811/.6—dc23

Dedication

*To the One who turns my mourning into dancing
and withholds no good thing.*

Contents

Bones and Flesh / 9
Moments / 10
Reflections Of A Rockstar / 11
The Ghost In My Reflection / 12
Pieces / 13
Tin-Plate Silhouette / 14
Eternal / 16
Watching the Storm / 19
Moments In the Desert / 20
Lone Bird / 23
Fading (song) / 25
Becoming My Mother / 27
She Never Knew She Was Beautiful / 30
The After / 31
Overcome / 34
Resolved / 35
Watching From Above / 37
Mirror Reflections / 38
Relief In the Dawn / 40
Then You Came / 41
Home With You / 42
After the Fire / 46
Brothers / 48
Winter Willow / 50
Turning Over A New Leaf / 51
The Dream / 52
Gray Storm / 54
This Faded Leaf / 56
Axis / 57
Horizon / 59
Like Water / 60
Surrender (song) / 62
I Am the Storm / 64
When Sunlight Shattered Midnight / 66
Winter's End / 67
Silence / 68
Haven By the Sea / 69
Leap / 70
To Feel You / 71

Red / 72
Choice / 73

Author Profile / 74

Bones & Flesh

I look at the bones of the world,
the limited scope of vision through which we see.
There are words for these things,
phrases we use, a language of the physical surface.
But the pulse of our being lies deep
beneath a veneer of polish and shine.
We think, we feel,
we have our being in souls of clay
molded by the vibrations of change and circumstance,
by the ocean of our souls that breathes and dreams,
that imagines and feels.

The language of the soul is a symphony,
liquid notes that create a harmony we meld with
that lifts us and moves us forward.
But how can we express the inexpressible?
How do we give flesh to our tangible world?
How can we feel what is so far beyond that solid language
we've created to explain a shell?

Music touches the heart of our beings, beauty draws it forth.
But perhaps the pen, being mightier than any sword,
dips its ink in our hearts' blood and pours it forth.
It is a compass, a microscope, a window.
All things and surface nothings blended together to sing,
to record, to remember, to experience the moments again,
to pour forth the feelings best left unexpressed to any ear,
to expose the poison in the veins of our souls
and cleanse it from the past and its many sorrows.

The pen gives us a voice to herald the beauty
of a glorious world both without and within.

May we always give voice
to the listening ear of our souls.

Moments

An acorn falling into a pond, the ripple it creates,
the tear that slips down a cheek, the smile that stills its flow,
the laughter that disturbs the quiet air,
the breath that catches in your throat,
and the warmth that follows the sunrise.

There. Gone. Come again.
The ticking of the clock,
the chiming of the hour,
the shifting in the air.

The touch, the release,
the melting of one gaze into another,
the silence, the waiting, the knowing in the stare.
Nothing alone, but love in the collection.

There. Gone. Come again.
The ticking of the clock,
the chiming of the hour,
the shifting in the air.

We are a collection of moments that gather
into hours, to days, to years,
raindrops caught in a bucket, poured out to create a lifetime.
Small flashes of insignificance breathed into beauty,
echoed in song, each fading to match each birth.

There. Gone. Come again.
The ticking of the clock,
the chiming of the hour,
the shifting in the air.

Reflections of a Rockstar

I am the ghost in the mirror
who seeks only to find her substance
in an insubstantial, colorless world
of false bravado, sex and rock n' roll.

When I still retained some flesh, I longed to be a mist
that could not hurt, could not fear, could not feel.
Now I look back with longing.

I once sought the darkness, to hug my knees and cry,
protect myself from the pain.
Now I long for the light to warm the ice in my bones.

What do we become when
we deaden ourselves to the world?
Of what substance are empty words,
sleepless nights, alcohol fogged days?

As we grew, we replaced sugar for powder,
sugar rush for adrenaline rush,
backyard birthday parties for nightclub parties,
nursery rhymes for the overwhelming tide of the crowd.

Realization, fill me with substance again,
thaw these chilly bones,
breathe life into shriveled lungs,
and part the storm clouds again.

The Ghost In My Reflection

I press my palm to the mirrors cool surface.
Flat and smooth it fits to my skin.
Frost condenses onto smoky reflections,
silver pearls against the light of sky and stormy sea.

Jaded, you called me,
but I am alive and paper-thin,
innocent and naïve.
But I've seen too much,
and I'm still alone.

Who would believe in this world of secret shadows?
Who would know the whispers as they're told?
First you in the world in front,
then me in the netherworld behind,
the same, yet different, the twin and the reverse.

I am across the doorway to the unknown,
you are planted in the sod of the certain.
You look to today, I am lost in yesterday,

Pieces

I stare numbly at the pieces, of who I was, who I am,
at the prospect of who I yet may be.
All the divine of purpose, of hope,
the light that persists behind the watery clouds,
catches in a silver pool at my feet, colors
reflecting the light of a thousand suns,
shattered shards of recollection and dream.

Beauty, fickle friend, you allow yourself to be broken.
Hope, you condescend to grief, and time,
you relentless sentinel, you march on
as inexorably as always, a soldier,
undiminished, undefeated, ever true.

By you, my trembling faith, I lift my eyes.
By you I dare to hold on, while falling, spinning, turning,
taking my bruises as they come.
My flickering candle holds its flame,
ballasted by your foundation.

Many battles beneath many skies I have seen,
many defeats have scarred my face.
But ever- pressing on as the screen moves forward I step,
I rise a little higher every time I get backup from falling.

Tin-Plate Silhouette

Amber skies with dark silhouettes,
the ghostly remains of memory,
tin-stamped and pressed into bronze.
A plate that captures moments,
pages in an endless book,
a tirade called 'life-time'.

Far from me, your eyes hold me still,
rock the foundations of my soul.
And this foundation, how easily it crumbles,
then rebuilds itself in rewind.

Ever, in the secret little corners of my mind,
you linger like dust heated by sunlight,
on a window-frame of long ago,
the same dust that hovered like pixie magic,
in the air around us as we danced.

I begged you to stay, to let this magic be enough,
but your eyes wandered to brighter lights,
magic that held more glitter.
I begged you to remember who you were
when we were young.

Your smile was too brilliant
to be forever held in my eyes alone,
your dreams too big to be contained.
So the amber skies began to darken,
so the silhouette of two became one.

What once was a love we could take back to childhood,
swings rhythmically passing innocence away
      like a pendulum,
forward, backward, echoing laughter
as I flew high to land in your arms,
and you dropped to the grass entwined in my arms.

Now I see you as a glistening mirage,
same face, same eyes, same magnetic charm,

but a different finish,
an airbrush to cover the imperfections,
the flaws I love because they make you who you are,
and your eyes are haunted when they brush mine,
                      remembering...

Eternal

I thought perhaps it was enough to dream,
and for some time, as a child, it was.
But children grow up, and adults grow older.
Now I reek of the potential never spent.
only thirty-six years of age,
no great age to the eyes of most men,
but my childhood withered and spent,
my youth degraded almost into nothingness.

Still I carry on.
What more can mothers do?

I dream, I while away, I hope, for a tomorrow
that is not so bleak as today,
still wanting for more for my son,
than what I myself have known.
If I'm honest, still wanting for more for myself,
than what I myself have known.
But how can one measure hope?

Do you measure hope by the spoonful,
as sugar dropped in a steaming cup?
Do you measure it by the shadows that fall
outside a window whose sill is worn with care?
Do you measure it by the years,
by the tears that have fallen
with no gentle fingers to brush them away?
Would you, can you, measure it by weight?
Were I to measure mine
it would make any scale break,
it would harden coal into diamond.

And against the bright backdrop of sky,
hope's wings brush the clouds,
and sing in a clarion anthem to the heavens.
What dreams, what imaginings have come and gone?
Were I to try and count them myself,
I am sure I would be vastly perplexed.

Hope if given a face, a definition, could be a taunt
or it could be a torture.
It could be considered bread dangling from a string
above a starving man.

Until its culmination, until the fruit has gone
        over-ripe on the tree,
until the last sweet drops of longing have run out,
hope hovers like a bleeding butterfly.
It flies, it hovers, it alights always just out of reach,
it makes your bones ache as you weary
with every passing day
waiting for things to change.
And the only thing to change is you,
your hair a little grayer,
your eyes a little more dull
for their wearing, for their tears.

My eyes are good, I know it.
My heart is good, I know that even more.
My instincts, the sharp wit of my pen,
all are gifted with heart.
And yet the dullness lingers, ever the poverty lengthens,
ever my tears grow dry.
I wonder if my crime was so great
it warrants this purposeless toil.

When out of this darkness, a faint light
will show the pathway to strength, to gain,
as something within me swells, and brightens
and longs to blossom in unending spring.
There my eyes beckon, there my heart sings,
there my hands ever will reach,
and by hope's fluttering wings
grasp what was so evasive, so slippery before,
as the world turns on its axis from shadow to sun.

The fickle eyes of the storm that tears the skies apart,
then washes them slowly clean,
and bears a lullaby on swollen breezes

heady with the scent of spring.
Where on God's green earth are you heading
when kissing long midnight goodbye?
Like a pendulum counting out days,
I know that you, hope, will spring eternal.

Watching the Storm

Sitting on the edge of the world watching heat lightning
beneath a darkened sun,
thunder rolling like an ocean in my chest.
The time it was, the time it seems,
the time it yet may be.

An abyss of choices on either side
 of a chasm my dreams create.
To follow, to lead, to be buffeted
like a leaf in a tempestuous wind.

Oh to be a flower carried away,
sunk quietly into river silence,
rather than the mast on an unsinkable ship,
that bears its face to the storm.

And I your watch-mate, your intercessor by night,
your lowly benefactor by day,
just a puff of fog in a sky full of pearly clouds.

I stand watch by your bedside.
I cry into your pillow at night.
I watch as your goodness fades away,
as the star becomes you,
becomes glitter, becomes light,
where once it had been only warmth.
Such shallow comfort you now keep.

Like a candle beneath a blazing sun melting away
by the same heat that sustains you.
What is worse than becoming a martyr to your own cause?
What is worse than becoming what you hate?

So I sit here on the edge of your world,
watch the storm rage from above.
The thunder rolls in my chest like the sea,
The time it was, the time it seems,
the time it yet may be.

Moments In the Desert

I.

The dune rolls over like an hourglass spilling her jewels,
fine grains, a course gritty curtain like billowing white sails.
It must be rough to refine, to scour the rough edges
of this wandering spirit,
who came for trial by fire and sea.

Endless waves of desolation, wisdom a cool kiss
in the darkness of this soul,
that catches and tugs at the tattered cloak of who I am,
who I once meant to be,
chills me to the marrow of the scattered bones of my dreams.

Buried in the sand like forgotten treasures,
their edges dull and smooth from the constant wearing,
a brittle skeleton lying in wait for me to collect up
the moments of hours of days,
I had long since forgotten...

Time fades in this place, stretches on and on,
scant remainders of white days, cooling to silver-blue nights,
the diamonds on the crystal waters of mirage,
the shattered tears cast down from the desert moon.

My hoarse voice to cry out for acknowledgment,
my red eyes to regard the brutal sun.
The phantom whispers on the breeze to echo in my ears
and taunt my fevered mind,
alone again with all that I dare to dream.

A person who was strong, resilient, brave,
who wanted nothing more than what you forgot and forgave,
to pass into shadows long forgotten by man,
to be the perfect stranger regarded by all.

Yet empty is the cup that runneth over gifted by a bitter world.
"Such anger. You are your father's son."

II.

The voice that still whispers, faint and distant,
over empty white hills,
somehow resonates deep within my spirit.
How it calls, how it draws, how it hungers for me,
how persistent its plea for surrender.

Giving up the old life, shedding skin like A cobra in its season,
letting go of the dried husk of my desire,
to be what *You* want, not what I will.
How tragic a price was paid for my pride.

I beg for the pardon of a Father who bleeds,
who gave and forgave for me,
but swim my way through the anger, the bitterness,
that clouds my searching eyes.
How could You be both loving and blind?

To the agony, the endless groans
of a world gone hard and cold,
that leaves the children abandoned and used,
broken as the glass of crystal seas,
that smile and laugh and reach out helplessly for me.

Faith is the only way the blind can truly see,
not as a fanciful hope, or a dream;
but in the character of one who suffered as much
as any fragile creature of mortality can endure.
He was crushed too for my wickedness.

When I don't understand, I can only reach out,
as those who depend upon me, reach for breath,
reach in thirst, for sweet water, though a vagrant hope.

III.

'Speak to me. I am speaking still.
'Where are you?'
I am here. Always.

'Why are you so hard to find?'
Because you look in the wrong places.
'Why must they suffer? Why can't You care?'
I do care. I send them you.
'One man can't do it all.'
He can if he abides in me.
He can do more than he ever dreamed.
And you are not alone. Never alone.

Listen to the voice that sings,
when the hot, dry breath of the desert whistles past.
Listen to the music in the parts of you that seem hollow.
      Fill them with me.
Listen to the voice that comes through,
that seems insistent, and just a little mad.
Is foolishness too hard a price to pay for truth?

What is your city like?
"Dirty and corrupt. But alive, very alive."
And so much you have grown.
But still, I love you at your dirtiest and your most alive.
And the cleansing only comes through me.

Am I really so hard to relate to, son?
Talk to me as you would any other.
I am here, I am waiting.
My arms are open. My cup does not run dry.

Lone Bird

I sit stationary on my high branch
too overwhelmed to open my beak.
I stare into a cacophony of chaos, feathers jostling on wires
that cross like stitch-work across the quilt-square fields.
The velvet light of the sun casts shadows
of the fluttering wings,
of a thousand cackling crows,

They caw their venom, their taunting, their laughter,
they attack and they land stolidly.
They undulate on the same rhythm be it near or farther on.
Their throaty voices ring hollow, as much as they try
to fill the silence with words, with power, with noise,
try to fill the empty with endless debate.

Is there even one among them who still remembers
what they are fighting for?
Is there one among them who has not betrayed their ideals
for the indignance of an opposing thought,
the weapons of a warfare that will never cease,
cast broken pieces of others' lives on the ground at their feet.

What do I know of the world?
What do I know of the wind that pesters,
that blows a torrent against the very skies
and scatters all like confetti into the darkness?
What do I know of a language
that can only shout and never calm,
words that can only incite, never placate.

I may be a child tossed into a world too big,
with dreams too grand and glorious for little me.
I may be the observer who can only stare and cry
as the days tear each other apart,
before night ushers the terrible silence
of bewilderment, of confusion, of despair.
Where can I go to block out the voices,

that shout and riot even in my own mind?

Burying my beak in my breast
as shadows softly fall to cloak me
in this lonely corner of the world.
I spurn the role of observer, of recorder,
of the quiet pawn to their unending game.
Where have all the champions gone,
who gather wayward wanderers in?
Where are the heroes who let none drown in the endless sea?

'Rally to me! To me! And lay down your weary head.
Even soldiers can cry when their fingers are numb,
from the bite of the tempestuous winds, that carry you far,
and lay you again against my chest.'

Fading (Song)

VERSE 1

From the corner of your eye
we see the world
and the world is fading.
The world is slowly fading.

The colors of 'hello'
that lit up your skies.
We watch the moonlight glow
as 'hello' becomes goodbye.

CHORUS

And nothing lasts forever
though we hold on while we may.
We dream of lost tomorrows
while we cling to yesterday.
We cling to yesterday

VERSE 2

From the memories in your eyes
we watch the movie.
We watch it slowly playing.
Like a playlist it's repeating.

Worked too hard for too long.
Worked to beat the run.
The run from endless dreaming.
The living and the breathing.

CHORUS

And nothing lasts forever
though we hold on while we may.
We dream of lost tomorrows
while we cling to yesterday.
We cling to yesterday.

BRIDGE

I don't know how we've come to this.
I don't know when or why.
I only know we've come too far.
to wish it all away
To wish it all away.

VERSE 3

From the smile on your face
we hear the song.
We hear the music fading.
We hear it softly fading.

The laughter in your eyes
was a once upon a time:
As the sunset fills your skies.
As dreams softly say goodbye.

CHORUS

And nothing lasts forever
though we hold on while we may,
We dream of lost tomorrows
while we cling to yesterday.
We cling to yesterday.

But we'll hold on while we may.

Becoming My Mother

I

I am the sum of all my fears.
The images I see in the mirror shatter,
scatter into chips of memory, reflection and useless grit.
Be they pitiful or mighty, those memories are mine,
closeted alone in my head, seen through my eyes.
I can see through no other...

Pictures on a wall, glistening in the sun one moment,
shadowed by the silence in the next.
Lives I've lived, places I've been, people I've met.
They are me but broken into bite-sized nuggets,
happiness, joy, and sadness,
little tiles pieced together into a complicated mosaic.

II

Curlers in my hair at night,
ribbons to bind them in the morning.
My brothers are rowdy, they play rough games.
Why can't I play too?
I am a young lady, rough and tumble with scabs on my knees
beneath the hem of a homemade dress.
I am angry like a champagne bottle about to burst its cork.
I am fiery like the embers that glow from the campfire
erected on this family trip.
I am moody, I am happy, I am sad.
I am a fighter. But I am all of a girl at heart.

Tying up my saddle-shoes, perfume and lace
and penny candy at the store,
Sweet, sticky cherry melting in my mouth,
an ice cream soda from the fountain in the square,
the pharmacy and pill bottles, blue and green and white.
The smell of moth balls, cedar, turtle wax, and shoe leather,
my childhood, in a black and white photograph,
etched into time, into my memory, frayed at the edges.

Playing tag in the orchard as the sun began to set,
the willow tree is base, but not the willow tree!
The willow tree can't be safe!
I picked my own switches from its wrap-around branches,
when father was angry...

A figure in the doorway after mama had said goodnight.
It was not daddy. I am half awake.
I saw, but didn't see the stranger taking my sister from the room.
It was just a dream. Not real.
My sister's eyes skirt mine the next morning.
The dream comes again.

Bright and bold my future loom,
beehive hair and poodle-skirts,
Elvis and the Beatles on the radio.
My older sister had the most dates,
but all of mine were taller!

III

That was not me. That is not me! It won't BE me!
Breathe. stay the course.
In... out...
Fight the good fight.
Sigh. Cry.
But don't give up.

IV

Raindrops on my windowpane, the smell of wet grass
and wood softened by the sun,
the TV in the background chattering
its canned laughter and assurances.
You were gone. Had been for a long time.
You weren't coming back.
I was here alone against the world.
My world was a colorful landscape of make-believe
locked inside a squawking box. It was real to me.

Better than what life had shown itself to be.
My dreams were bigger than the moon.
The time it was. The time it would yet be...

V

I was not a fool, but a fool I acted
because I deserved a fool's fate.
So I ran away because I wanted to see
if You would come after me.
You didn't. You let me run...
But you were waiting there with open arms
when I came staggering home.

VI

Now I gnash my teeth and fight against
the reflections that war inside of me.
The broken shards are jagged and tear my insides apart.
But they are toughening the fragile flesh to scars.
Who I was. Who I am. Who I yet may be....

Breath. Stay the course.
In... out...
Fight the good fight.
Sigh. Cry.
But don't give up.

I am a warrior, just as she was a warrior before me,
and I will not give in to despair.

She Never Knew She Was Beautiful

Her smile was like the sun;
it chased away every shadow,
her laughter like butterflies rising in jubilation.
While clumsy in her speech, she made friends
as consistent as the sunrise.
While unorganized and packrat-like, her elegance was in her faith.
Bruised hard by life, she punched back at its blows.
And she persisted when all goodness was gone around her.
Childish, but breathing innocence,
blinded to a world she could not fathom,
and holding tight to what she knew, what she loved.
Chained to her sickness,
she had a heart that would melt the sun.

She had no idea she was beautiful.

The After

Then you closed your eyes...
But just before you did, I thought you might have smiled,
as though accepting the end with perfect grace,
as though grateful your pain was finally at an end.
But I know you better... or do I?

In that final moment, the infinitesimal moment it took
to exhale your last breath,
as the lighted tunnel quickly began to compress and shrink,
you chose to move forward, to pass beyond our world,
to whatever lies behind, that thin, but elastic, membrane,
traversable only to the dying.

Before the tunnel closed behind you forever,
was your last thought of heaven?
Of the life you lived here?
...was it of me?

When I was brought forth from you screaming
into the cold light of the world,
you saw my wrinkled purple face,
the misshapen, alien skull
and pronounced me beautiful
as only you could see.
And as you lay here now, waxen and still,
I pronounce you beautiful,
as only I can see.

Your life was full of wounds and scars,
but also full of the sunshine of your smile,
the illuminated chatter of your laughter.
When all the world tried to hold you back,
you fought forward and you won. You won.
You fought through both the pain and the pressure,
you fought through illness and through
the cold tongue of discouragement.
You fought through abuse and physical restraint
Just to breathe, just to be.

And I remember the moments we shared running in the park
as I swung high up into the air,
and you caught me on the back-swing
and pushed harder as I demanded more.
When I woke in the night, my stomach a tumble,
my body in distress, my muscles aching
from the forced exit of my inner being,
you soothed my sore muscles with a touch,
 you held back my hair, you fretted with me
and cried along with me to show your love.

When I grew and determined never to cry again,
never to allow myself to love,
you lamented the foolish notion of becoming impenetrable,
of not allowing hurt in, but not allowing love in either.
And when my reckless dreams and shattered hopes
came crashing down, when I refused to cry out loud,
it was you who shed the tears. For me.

When I made my mistakes and lived an unstable life,
when my plans inevitably came crashing down around me
like a house of cards, you let me make the mistakes...
(Did you really have a choice?)
But you were also there to love me
when my deal was struck, the game set,
and there were no more cards left,
to deal or to flutter down.

When at last I proceeded forward with a little more wisdom,
a few more scars to remind me of the salt
that had burned in my wounds, you cheered from the sidelines
and uttered your prayers of thanksgiving even though
I could not bring myself, in my pride, to admit you'd been right.

And when the doctor gave you the news...
it wasn't you who cried. It was me.
You were frightened, as anyone would be,
but you comforted my concerns with your smile,
and never allowed the disease to take who you were from you.
So your journey kept you here with us
instead of within the storming vortex of defeat.

But that was before...
And now I wonder where exactly you are,
what your mind is thinking of,
and if you can still see me, hear me,
touch me when I am asleep.
Are you conscious in another place,
consumed by beauty I cannot imagine?
Or are you merely asleep awaiting the call
to awaken on the last day?
Do you talk to me in my dreams
when my unconscious mind returns home,
to where I grew up beneath your vigil?
Do you see that every honeysuckle
and every hummingbird cannot help but remind me of you?

Are you behind the distant stars I study
in the lonely heart of the night?
Or do you wait... do you wait for me?

Is your current home so grand you cannot spare a visit?
Not even a hello from the other side?
Or are you on the sidelines still cheering me on
and celebrating my victories,
when all I can do is cry that your silhouette has disappeared?
You used to tell me, when you were gone,
you didn't want me to weep any tears,
no crying, no hesitation, no regrets.
But that leaves me here without the warmth of your embrace,
without the beloved stubbornness of your face.
The world is so cold without your fire sometimes...

You used to tell me you had no doubt
one day I would succeed,
that one day my blossoming star would shine,
and others would come to know the beauty in me
that you could see. But that was before...
And I am stuck here now wondering
you're imagining,
In the After...

Overcome

Oh to hope for a solvent prayer,
capable of uttering every thought,
untwining the tangled mess of thorns I have become.
How can I ask for absolution when none is sure to come?
Part of me is alive and longing,
part of me has died with you.

I sing to the heart of me a song of chaste rebuke,
begging the low-born phoenix to rise,
shake away the ashes of my grief,
and all that I would cling to holds me near
even when I cannot feel its touch.

Excusing the wind that blows me apart
because the pieces of me are too fragile to resist.
And I, light and heavy at the same time scatter apart
and sink into this endless sea.

Lifting my head to glimpse the gold,
the thin band along the horizon.
Dawn chases the darkness, this shimmering thread,
the parts of me that are broken will be made new
as I trust, I run after,
I collapse into You.

Resolved

Who was I then?
When my eyes wanted wonder and found dismay.
When they were struck by beauty,
then followed after with despair.

I was young then,
untethered by practicality, undeterred by restraint.
It was easier to know then
what was right, what was wrong,
but not nearly so easy to know what to expect.
I wasn't so jaded by life, but softer
and more fragile for its beatings

No longer a child, but never quite wise,
I begin to know where the hurt stops and where I begin
to fight for hope instead of passing the victory to despair.
It doesn't matter quite so much what others think or expect
as I've grown into my faults and begun to celebrate
my peculiar brand of cleverness.

Still, between then and now, I've held onto tomorrow,
collected the raindrops of yesterday
instead of allowing them to spill all over the ground.
The scars have formed my reflection,
but they do not define it,
nor will they rob me of my dreams.
There is a fierce beauty in resilience
that far outweighs resignation.

In quietness I fight.
In quietness I both seethe and sing.

With loud shouts I will voice what my heart would utter.
With brilliant smiles I will light up the world
that's ever danced just beyond my reach
and clasp it to my breast in defiance,
and in triumph hold its vibrant hues to my soul.
I will shed no tears for time spent

and bear fulfillment upon bruised breast,
gently brushing aside fury with fingers unwound from fists

What strength I had given to sadness, I will reap in joy.
If only...one day more...and one day more.

Watching From Above

Ever-watching from above.
Wise, observant, benevolent.
Do you still see my tears?
Do you still reach to hold me
when the nights grow long and cold and lonely?

I have fallen and You have lifted me back up
a thousand times and more,
yet, still I walk on wobbly legs, uncertain as a toddler
peering out at a mysteriously beautiful
and unimaginably cruel world.
And You give no answers to my questions.
Perhaps I ask the wrong questions.
Perhaps I should not ask at all.

You saw my first steps,
you wiped away my first tear.
And You have seen me grow, and blossom.
And now I begin to fade...

I am still with You.
You are always with me.
And until at last the heavy blue clouds above
close over my weary eyes
I will trust You are the God who sees,
who knows, who loves me.
Though answers are too soft to hear
and scattered like confetti in a garden full of colors.

Mirror Reflections

Just before the dawn, before the world begins to stir,
I draw near the reflective glass
shuddering with trepidation.
There is no enemy greater than that
which is created and birthed within me.
I look at myself clearly, all honesty and brutality.

I am me, and I am brilliant. I am light.
I am softness and strength.
I am power and fragility.
I am a glass dagger, sharp in my approach,
but brittle and easily broken.
The first birds begin to sing,
and I am a whiny little girl afraid of her own shadow.

I am the arbiter of light and darkness,
a frail shadow cast against the wall of my own fate.
Dreams trickle down the window like rain,
jagged lines these sky-tears make, yet smooth to the touch,
like the edges of the dagger I hold close to my heart.
If death comes to those dreams, it will be by my own hand.
A terror I am to my younger self, an assassin of the promise,
yet I hold my weapon closely, weighing it in my hands.
The story is of the young girl staring back at me in the glass
and how her skin has wrinkled in the sun
of unrealized potential till she stands as her own hunter
debating her choices to pursue her heart's desire,
or to turn away and forget innocence evermore.
She is, I am, the story never written,
the dreamer waiting for the dream
and lost in her own ambition.

And yet... and yet, I am stronger for my weaknesses,
hardened by the hurt.
I am a rock petrified by the mighty waves
that cast their punches against my sides.
A sharp arrow to pierce the hardest of steel
and shatter into silence once its deeds are done.
A pebble in a stream worn smooth from constant abrasion.

The story is, as the story goes...
The two images in the glass begin to merge.
I am none of, some of, nothing
and all parts of me.

Relief In the Dawn

The young sun touches my skin,
thaws away the cold of night.
Awakes the spirit in me to rest from the endless fight.

You are, my friend, your own enemy and closest friend.
You try to control your destiny,
but float in the current, flutter in the breeze,
ever wavering, ever weakening in the rising tide
of who you are and yet to be.
You are like a butterfly who can't decide where to land,
above the dancing sunlight, over the water.

So let me breathe in the freshness of dawn,
rest from the struggle with self,
my powerful weakness and feeble strength.
My feet are light on the clouds
and heavy on the cold ground.
So I hover, on the thin membrane between,
gazing longingly at the sun.

Let me remember how I rose
on the smoke that ascended from burning dreams
rather than the ashes that remain.
Let me remember the quiet of the night
rather than the fear that clawed at me in the dark.

Morning is the respite between darkness and light,
between struggle and rest.
So I soar on swelling breezes as dawn stains the sky
like colored ink bleeding onto a blank black page.
I trace the fading stars with my fingertip
and draw a rose with their silver light,
twisting the silver leaves between my fingers.

This is my offering, my contribution to the world
for one morning's relief from my mind.
The old moon winks as it melts into the blue
and hides behind the sky until night calls once again.

Then You Came

I am the owl in the desert
sifting through the shadows above these ruins,
resting on the bleached bone tree,
trembling at the deep beneath its feet,
hiding under the vastness of the stars above.
And I am lost. And I am alone.

I listen to the sand reply to the breeze,
the soft hiss as it shifts over the waves
of this dry and barren sea.
I sink into the silence of blue and gray
and dream of waters far away.
I was… I am… I…was.

Then you came…

I am the robin on the rooftop
singing in the sunlight above these green, verdant fields,
resting on the budding branch of orchard trees.
And as I press my ear against your chest,
I tremble at the deep beneath my cheek.
And I am found. And 'I' becomes 'we'.

We behold the red horizon, the lightning and the heat,
the raindrops that draw rivers in the sand,
then increase and dissolve it away.
The clouds cool the fury, but keep the passion
and the intensity of your gaze.

Home With You

I

I stumble along the worn sidewalk,
every day as the one before;
My footsteps have chiseled a path in the dirty stone.
The smog smudges the city line, smears my face
as I pass an arm across my sweaty brow.
It stains even the graffiti that shouts out its defiance,
beneath the tunnel, alongside the stairs.
I hear the thunder of a million feet
plodding the same weary rhythm,
the roar of cascading waters
against this decaying cataract of slum.

The repetition abrades my nerves,
rubs them raw, then numb.
My years and my tiredness vex me.
My mind and ambitions are
as alive as they were in my youth,
but my body lags behind.
And my head, that beleaguered mind, begins to wander.
And though I know it's banality, it's fixed position in cliche,
I turn my thoughts to my childhood...

II

The depravity of the city alleyways was unknown.
The sound of gunfire and mothers sobbing unheard.
Our green then was not money, not the platitudes of greed.
It was the sea of grass waving in the field beside our home.
Our gold was the sun in the morning
as it caught the wheat beneath the morning mist
and sang to us full and ripe in the fall.
There our nights were full of story-time and rainbows,
catching fireflies in the summer dusk,
lullabies and sweet dreams.
How I long to return to that sweeter time,
walk the weedy wheel-ruts of the dirt lane,
and laugh like we used to laugh in our youth

as we played hide-and-seek in our safe neighborhood.
We played until the streetlights were lit
and returned sweaty, tired and satisfied
to the unlocked doors of our homes.
On Sunday nights we were sticky
with our melted ice-cream cones
and wild blackberries stained our cheeks.

III

And now alone again, I walk back my steps and stare
at the new face looking back at me,
suddenly alive and suddenly dear.
And the tumult of the city-streets
fade into music-filled midnights,
fire dances at crowded tables
and fairy lights glistening overhead.
Long drives and rambling thoughts
we treasure re-living and re-learning ourselves.
Separate for one lifetime,
and now never apart in this next,
as sunset stains the river into our love-song.
Longer drives and longer kisses and each city-drive
that turned chaos into melody.
And suddenly the skies of hope are opened
and the threatening clouds make way for dawn
as together we join the silhouettes of trees
on new, but somehow familiar country lanes.
I breathe the vision of our future together,
and no day is ever quite the same.

IV

The green scent of fresh-cut grass,
long-needled pines along the lane,
the pond a silver coin suffused with morning mist.
The old dock creaks in the cool air
and replaces the splinters
we'd sanded-out the spring before.
With faded eyes it winks in the morning sun.
'See you again next year!'
The fish nibble at the dragonflies

that laze above the surface
and ripples reach out their circular waves
to reach the nearest shore.

Leaves that have dusted the stone fire-pit
curl in the remaining smoke.
It's embers ever-burn and hunger
for more of the trees confetti
to toss up in clouds of autumn spice,
to mix with the chimney plume above the roof,
above the gabled shutters of our quiet place,
our sanctuary against the windy nights.

I dance my pen against a new page and smile as I write.
I have not the confidence of Whitman,
perhaps once the self-loathing of Brutus.
I strive now for the patience of Eliott
as he penned his greatest laments
while embracing the beauty of his pain.
You make a blank page come alive
with figures of ink, of graphite and lead.
I ponder the jonquil stone, the pearl,
and the sapphire and arrange them with care
to sparkle best in the sun
while you tend the succulents on the porch
and stretch your growing vines.

And as we curl together like damp puppies behind a stove,
the dry rattle of the most stubborn of leaves overhead
seems to us a symphony. And we've laid aside
the fevered excitement of unfilled dreams
for this, for peace, for our togetherness, for forever.

And you are my safe place, my warm hearth.
You are home where I am a cat that will sleep blissfully
in the embrace of the autumn sun
as the last fading rays of day melt over the worn fence
like honeyed syrup and brown sugar.
We smell the aroma of over-ripe apples
in their bushels in the barn
as we look through the glass at the quieting world

content beneath our quilt.

Never mind the silvering hair,
the way our bones creak in the drafts,
the way our breath sputters in startled clouds
in the chilly morning to come.

We are together. We are beautiful.
We are far from the city lights
and never nearer to our eternal Home.

After the Fire

With bated breath, I watch the flames
climb up the trellis and dance merrily towards the sky.
Hellfire, not warm firelight stoked her fury.
Vengeance, not comfort motivated the red embers
to grow, to grow... like a cancer that could not be willed away.
And like the aforementioned, she rent her destruction
tearing out the pure foundations of home
instead of bathing us in the pure succor of comfort
to ward off the cold air
as by the hearth we'd spent so many nights.

***

Now the hearthstones are blackened and the embers cold,
smitten into silence by the fires long fury
and the fingers of cruelty
on whose brow she'd rent her carnage.

***

I kneel to touch my fingertips to the black ash,
and my fingers encounter death.

Soot smears my skin like the blackened tears of one
who has lost it all in the space of a dragon's breath.
So far away like echoes from a forgotten night
are the memories of laughter and whispers of life.
What once was pure is now darkened and desiccated
in the light of a pale, watery sun.

***

To live and love I have known.
Those little flickers of life, of family and security.
To lose, to die, to grieve,
know it's agonies and delights.

***

Yet from those ashes has risen a phoenix
whose colors will remain ever-bright.
Its plumage is vibrant and new in the jeweled eyes
that look up at me in wonder.

My own, many seedlings, my reflections were birthed
like the ripples in an ever-changing pond.
Thus the destructive rage of yesterday
did not, in the end, overcome the swells of hope.
Family triumphed over the onslaught of defeat.

Brothers

Brother 1:

You are my first, my only.
You are the beam of the earliest sunrise
and the warmth of its latest setting.
When I scurried about like an ant on steroids
among the cold concrete and even colder race to success,
you were the fresh, blushing violet
blooming through the cracked sidewalk
my feet had worn so many times.
You were the spring bursting through
the heavy gray clouds of winter.
You made the world new and pure and beautiful again,
gave me new meaning and a renewed purpose.
May I forever bow to the sweetness of your smile
as our aging leaves wilt beneath the searing heat
of time's ruthless, fading summer.

Brother 2:

I had forgotten then how new life used to be.
I held so tightly to squeaky new leather seats,
shoe polish, parted hair so sharp it could cut steel,
billboards with profits rising up
and grinding them ever higher.
Even when work ended and I came home to you,
I buried my head in newsprint and murmured empty platitudes
when you struggled to extract a soft word
from your spouse of stone.

I didn't even glance at the clean house,
notice the fresh scent of lemon and cedar
from your careful hands tending what success had wrought.
Not until you were lying there in that cold, sterile bed did I notice.
Not until I saw the light in your eyes had dulled
to a distant gray sheen did I care...
And then you were gone.

And the green-gold idol I had acquired
was too cold a comfort.

***

What was is no more.
What is can never come back.
Wrought from the warmth of adoration,
or pounded into the icy dollar he'd worshiped.
A brother. A son. Two men cut from the same cloth,
but ripping the seams apart to form two different blankets.
A blanket of warmth and comfort.
An impenetrable, cold blanket of snow.

Winter Willow

Tinseled tresses swaying ponderously,
a slow pendulum ticking out the minutes of winter.
Long, jeweled strands glisten in the cold, white sun.
These arms have embraced the summer
and whispered their melodies to lovers secreted below.

They have been the lash to children
foolish or pitied in years past.
Now they rest as slumbering jeweled curtains
longing for Spring's thawing kiss.

Turning Over A New Leaf

The maple leaf trembled
waiting for the breeze to tip it up,
and over.

I admire its courage.

The Dream

There is a dream inside of me
that chases away all of my darkest nights.
It fights past every obstacle,
destroys every barrier,
and it keeps me alive.
It is the heat behind the spark kindled when I was born,
tended into a roaring fire by every year that passes.

This fire has scoured my spirit.
It has cleansed away the trauma and loss,
the heartache and grief that left me broken and bleeding.
But in that fragile place where I lay my head
on broken glass for a pillow
and cover myself with ashes for a blanket,
where I curl, naked and fetal
wishing to sink into the ground,
comes peace – with myself and my world
and all the ruins around me.
Comes joy for all the blessings that pain has and will bring.
Comes the passion that blazes bright,
fuels the bonfire within me as it sings!...
And as it cracks into tiny pieces that are flung at the sky,
wishes to rival the light of the stars!
I whisper into that tumult
that these glittering pieces of grit are mine.

I bathe in the warmth of that fire.
I dance with its hypnotic movements.
I rise like a startled band of butterflies
scattering upward into the sun!
And I am free.
And I allow myself,
despite all the chaos and crying around me,
to keep dreaming. To keep breathing.
To keep walking though there is a boulder on my back
and feel the strength in the burn that suffuses my muscles,
in the exhaustion that melts my bones.
I allow the power behind that fire to empower me.

You gave me this hope. You gave me this joy.
You gave me this promise to fulfill me,
to not abandon the work of Your hands.
And so I will be faithful, and I will follow
though the path ahead of me be dark
and shadowed by despair,
and though Your face grows hazy
in the light of a thousand storm clouds.
I will face the lightning with hope
and roar down the thunder with determination.
Because You are with me.
When I cannot see.
When I am broken and bruised,
when the night closes in and smothers me
and tosses me aside like a wilted leaf.
Because the thunder's fury broke over
You on a lonely hill
when mercy and justice collided
and were met beyond justice to grace.
And death became the conqueror no more that day.
You lead me beside still waters
but also lead me through a raging sea.
We walk in Your bleeding footsteps
even when the sharks are drawn to my progress
and the waves tower higher than the sky.

I will follow You through to the summit
though the wind pounds the mountains
and grinds their foundations to powder
because I know You guide my footholds
and hold my hands fast
when what I cling to must be only You above the void.

I pray these dreams will come alive! Will breathe! Will be…
I will shout down your sky with my hopes!
I will wrestle this angel to exhaustion!
I will die on this pyre of my ambition!
For the Almighty,
and for those, like me,
and the least of these.

Gray Storm

There is a gray storm
breaking the sky behind your eyes.
The jagged pieces pierce more than just you.
The distant images feel like a mirror reflecting back
my own darker days
when I was broken,
when I was alone despite the company.

It was my private war, but I was not a valiant soldier
and casualties amassed at my feet.
I remember the whispers I ignored
preferring my own bitter darkness.
I threw everything away I feared I'd lose.
I tore at my hair to rip the truth away,
and only gave myself these ragged scars,
broken nails and blemished skin.

I hated what I was,
So I turned myself into worse
To fit my self-perception of ugly,
Of what they thought of me.
The rain dampened the hair that hid my face,
And I cowered at the monster in my reflection.
I had created my own hell,
became a determined resident.
Better the hell I created
than the one they imposed on me.
I reached for my dreams
and grasped a nightmare instead.

And I see you...
like a paradoxical shadow, doing the same.

Freedom reaches out with both hands,
Holy, scarred and open, calling to you.
Redemption comes after your breaking,
for only breaking truly heals.

Peace He will give you,
not as the world gives and the world ignores.
Right and wrong are not fluid, or justice would not exist.
Boundaries you have torn down
have always been meant to protect.

Let go of your chains.
Don't wallow in slavery any longer.
Let the truth, the ONLY truth
set you free...

This Faded Leaf

I have a Father who makes the mountains tremble with His voice,
yet to stutter and to stumble is my choice.
Why is it so much easier to me
to cry in my own self-made agony?
Like a faded leaf I turn, I blow,
through the valleys to and fro
when there's a mountaintop you've created just for me.

I fill my head throughout the day,
afraid what the silence might say.
All the words become a drone.
And they are drowned out by the moan
of empty wind escaping me.
Oh God, rescue me!

And yet when silence comes,
I see the truth remains the same,
the finality and the desolation.
I must cry out Your name.

Be merciful to me, O God, be merciful to me,
for my soul takes refuge in You alone
And in the shadow of Your wings
I will make You my hiding-place
until this great trouble passes by.

Axis

I'm tortured by the incessant need to be where you are,
to breathe the cool spring air, and drink the gentle breeze.
To play among the fireflies in the meadows of my dreams,
And catch those dreams in bottles,
with no lid or hint of boundary.

I remember the summertime, the life, the green,
the growth, the stillness of the nights
as the cricket chorus rejoiced,
and the cicadas put them to shame.
When every day was sunshine and every tree part of the sky,
and spinning round and round
I drank in the euphoria of a world so grand and new,
And impossible was not a word we knew.

Blue swallowed every cloud, and we drowned in its deep,
as it spun above, beneath and over,
Like a playful gyro ball its compass always pointed north,
ror up, for glory, for hope.
What went up never had to come back down.
We were weightless, light, and free.
Life was beauty in its simplicity.
And you were its ballast, the constant, steady force
that kept the earth from swaying off its axis.

Now the daylight sways and cries,
unmoored, unanchored, wild in a hurricane of my grief.
Where does the circle go
when the beginning is lost in the end?
A sphere becomes an infinite invisible
spiraling into the unknown.

Heaven cries and Hades cackles,
the rain, the thunder's laughter.
Where is the world that was our genesis?
Where is the earth that became your bed?
Sleep, the paper layers of conscience
drifting you down to memory.
There, you never die.

And somewhere in my mind
you're as bright and fresh and new
As the spinning sky above when you were here.
Buried only in waking, so may I ever slumber
        and remember you.

Horizon

I stand here by the waves
looking to where sea melts into sky.
I dream, I believe, I die a little inside.

Between hope and loss,
between dreaming and awake,
I fall softly into the wide sky and Never-land.
Memories bleed into the water and I smile.
Another horizon beyond this shore.

Like Water

Pour me out like water.
I get back up and breathe harder.
Water ebbs and flows,
Deep and wide, it grows.

I writhe against the currents,
though their pull is strong.
I've been fighting far too long,
to keep alive what was
and let tomorrow change what does.

Let me dream it's still real.
It's easier to know than steal
moments that were hours that were days,
that were the ways we always were.

The dreams we made when young
don't always fit the fights we've won.
Let tomorrow bring the sun.
Pour me out like water,
I get back up and breathe harder.

Water ebbs and flows.
Deep and wide, it grows.
I see the treasures that were.
Addicted to the joy and pain,
afraid to look ahead and gain,
to see the promise and stay sane,
let go of the hurt and let it rain.

Let me dream it was real.
It's easier to know than steal
moments that were hours that were days,
that were the ways we always were.

The dreams we made when young
don't always fit the fights we've won.
Let tomorrow bring the sun.
Pour me out like water.
I get back up and breathe harder.

Water ebbs and flows.
Deep and wide, it grows.
I look ahead to the bright light.
I won't give in to this night,
I'll fight forward to the finish.
With You as my strength, I'll win this.

I'll move past the dying wish.
Let me dream it will be real.
It's easier to know than steal
moments that were hours that were days,
that were the ways we always were.

The dreams we made when young
don't always fit the fights we've won.
Let tomorrow bring the sun.

Surrender

VERSE 1

I wanna dive into the deep,
Swim in the widest sky,
Reach every star I've pondered from afar.
I wanna stand upon the heights,
Feel the weight of the breeze,
Fly against the currents of the wind.

CHORUS

Surrender
Surrender is the key
Not giving up, not giving in,
But letting Your will lead.

Surrender.
I lay down my weapons and take up Your shield,
I throw all my hope upon faith.

VERSE 2

I wanna revel in Your glory,
See you pass above the cleft,
I want to have the faith of Daniel in the den.

I wanna dream in technicolor,
Always be Your favorite son.
I want to vanquish every giant with a stone.
I want to read Your name in lightning,
As it arcs across the sky.
I wanna hear You in the thunder of the night.

So let me pour out every offering,
Every cry within my soul,
For every whispered prayer, I offer You.

CHORUS

Surrender
Surrender is the key,
Not giving up, not giving in,
But letting Your will lead.

Surrender
I lay down my weapons and take up Your shield,
I throw all my hope upon faith.

BRIDGE:

Oh, I'm lost in this ocean,
Floating on grace.
Lord, the peace You've given
Will brighten my face.
I don't care if I'm sinking,
As long as I'm drowning in You...

Surrender, I surrender to You.

Surrender, I surrender to You.

I Am the Storm

I fall into a deeper blue than sky, than sea, than stars,
the blue of twilight that melts into indelible dream.
I float, I sink, I drown...

Amber skies above a silver pond,
air heavy with pollen and seeds,
copper clouds with sepia linings
breathe in hot air like steam.

Children's laughter echoes nearby,
small silhouettes prance in the dark.
A forgotten doll in a grassy nest,
abandoned bicycle against a tree,
Dandelion seeds dance in an invisible breeze,
and the slow wink of fireflies
backdrop the lazily creaking tire swing.

The sky rumbles above the red horizon.
Lightning tears a jagged wound into the sky.
As memory stirs nostalgia into loss,
reminiscence to deep pain.

The curtains billow in, then out,
flutter like a wounded bird whose lost its way
as the wind quickens to precede the driving rain.
The children squeal as the first drops fall,
They scatter like butterflies toward the sky.
I cry for them not to go, to forever stay,
but they evaporate into the blackening sky,
sparks rising from a campfires flame.

I understand now that I am the storm
trespassing where I no longer belong.
I am the thunder as it rages evermore.
I am the clouds as they break into the rain,
that flow the summer sunshine all away.

Was it meant to be a moment,
a faint stirring in times all-seeing eye?
Do memories fade by candlelight while we quietly drift away?

Fly away...
Fly away.
Wings weren't meant to beat the dust
nor yesterday's golden suns to rust.

The wings of childhood were meant, after all else,
To fly away...

When Sunlight Shattered Midnight

Please let me breathe that summer breeze once more.
I don't mind re-living all the pain
cause the pain we felt made life feel much more real.
It made the joy much sweeter in the end.

All we had was our own separate dreams.
I looked to the moon, you followed me.
To you there was no moon without us,
for me, no one else I could trust.

But life became a game we could not win.
The truth became a lie; the world began to spin.
And all I thought I knew turned to dust.
The fire faded black; the shiny dreams began to rust.
When midnight shattered sunshine
in the garden that was us.

Alone became the place I went to play.
It swallowed every moment, every day.
And memories then were slices of the sky
that broke the moon and silenced every 'Why?'

Then I remembered what it was to pray.
The storm began to fade more every day.
And though the struggles happened just the same,
I'd learned my life was better off Your way.

It seems that I had never been alone,
I just turned my eyes away from Your throne.
And instead of being angry and turning me away,
You opened up Your arms for a new day.

I thought love was the great price I'd pay.
I learned to stand and walk, not run away.
And though the past still haunts me,
it's covered by Your grace.
And shame disappears with one look at Your face.
Your sunlight shattered midnight
in the garden that was us.

Winter's End

Magic takes the wings of winter
and transforms the cold, dead earth
into fairy tales and glitter,
masking the chill white blanket leaves behind.

Yet the night air is empty and hollow.
Unlike the passion of the rainbow,
winter's essence is so cold.
With dawn comes the relief after the long dark.

You are still amidst the frenzy,
yet restless in the heart of the flames.
The calm before the storm, and the rinsing of the sky after
blotting out the swollen ferocity of the thunderclouds.

Dandelion seeds and memories, the sweet heat
that makes the sugar cookies glisten.
The seasoning of the earth; the fire ignites the sky.

And life, so frail and gentle pushes stronger than the sea
in shoots of green, flowers of blue,
and waving oceans of fragrant color.

And the black is banished chased by sunshine
into some hidden place
where I no longer hide.

Silence

I am afraid of the silence
that presses down on me,
an oppressive force that expands the air
and pushes against me like thick water
revealing every scar, rubbing salt
in every wound
I have tried to hide.

Haven By the Sea

Sunflowers by the seashore,
the sun alighting both the same.
Silver glitter and golden smiles
dancing on the breeze.

Our little haven by the sea.

Leap

Leap into the sky
with wings that really fly.
Live there in the leap!
Never embrace the fall.
Allow the sun to heal.
Swim no longer
in the syrupy shadows of despair.

To Feel You

Sunlight streams through the wall of night.
Another day, another fight.
Still, I reach out for Your light.
And find You.
I find You.

When everything is so fast-paced,
it's too easy to forget Your grace.
Don't need success to fill this space,
just need to feel You.
To feel You.

Red

Red is the color of hurt shouting to be heard
against the busy background of your mind,
grief an ache that does not wane,
but is only learned to be tolerated and set aside.
When taken off its shelf, grief brings the beauty
of memory locked in bittersweet agony.

You are there. Always.
How it hurts to look at you in the silent images of my mind!
To know we are parted!
However temporarily, the seat is empty.
And that empty hole still tangles 'round my heart.

I could have made more time for you,
but didn't want to bring the knowledge into the open
that those moments were brief. Limited.
To bring it into the open would make it real,
something I could not accept.

And you knew I wouldn't believe it,
wouldn't let the door slam on hope.
You knew I couldn't let it be,
that I wouldn't let go.

My life has changed now.
It is settled, as you wanted.
I keep your memory alive.
I look like you, act like you,
some of the rougher edges refined.
But I haven't your smile, your laugh, or your spirit.

Forever is not forever where our hope lives on.
But until we meet again on heaven's sunny shores,
my heart burns red with the scar
of your memory.

Choice

A silver pond and a golden tree,
amber shadows of opportunity.
Pick your poison, so they say,
for good or ill, come what may.
Choose a scene with glittering eyes,
be sure your choice is shrewd and wise.
Looming shadows will dog your steps,
whether you've sighed or whether you've wept.
In faith your hopes must always rest
to be strong and to be blessed.
No choice is free from struggle or pain,
but right will bring the soothing rain.
And wounds will turn to memories made;
In peace your future plans are laid.
Beware the sin of vanity,
for if you stray, what will be, will be.

Author Profile:

Kaylie Rose is a poet by heart and has been writing in prose since the age of ten when her fifth grade teacher read her poem 'The Pond' to her class. She has also published a poem entitled 'Shadow On the Snow' in a poetry collection called 'Circular Whispers'. She lives with her husband, two stepdaughters and four cats in a small town in Pennsylvania.

www.ingramcontent.com/pod-product-compliance
Lightning Source LLC
Chambersburg PA
CBHW071253070526
44583CB00017B/2457